Marx Joyce
Abbott Hardy Machiavelli Chesterton Cooper Emerson Austen
Defoe Melville Montaigne Haggard Hugo
Christie Carroll Eliot Grimm
Stoker Molière
Wilde Maupassant Byron
Engels Schiller
Garnett Einstein Fitzgerald Smith
Goethe Hawthorne Kafka
Cotton Dostoyevsky Hall
Baum Kipling Doyle Willis
Leslie Dumas Henry Nietzsche
Flaubert Turgenev Balzac
Stockton Vatsyayana Crane
Burroughs Whitman Verne
Curtis Tocqueville Gogol Vinci
Homer Widger Tolstoy Busch
Darwin Thoreau
Potter Freud Zola Twain Plato Scott
Lawrence
Kant Jowett Stevenson Dickens
Andersen Cervantes Burton Hesse Harte
London Descartes
Poe Aristotle Wells Voltaire
Hale James Hastings Cooke
Bunner Shakespeare
Richter Chambers Irving
Doré Chekhov da Benedict Alcott
Swift Dante Shaw Wodehouse Pushkin
Newton

tredition®

tredition was established in 2006 by Sandra Latusseck and Soenke Schulz. Based in Hamburg, Germany, tredition offers publishing solutions to authors and publishing houses, combined with worldwide distribution of printed and digital book content. tredition is uniquely positioned to enable authors and publishing houses to create books on their own terms and without conventional manufacturing risks.

For more information please visit: www.tredition.com

TREDITION CLASSICS

This book is part of the TREDITION CLASSICS series. The creators of this series are united by passion for literature and driven by the intention of making all public domain books available in printed format again - worldwide. Most TREDITION CLASSICS titles have been out of print and off the bookstore shelves for decades. At tredition we believe that a great book never goes out of style and that its value is eternal. Several mostly non-profit literature projects provide content to tredition. To support their good work, tredition donates a portion of the proceeds from each sold copy. As a reader of a TREDITION CLASSICS book, you support our mission to save many of the amazing works of world literature from oblivion. See all available books at www.tredition.com.

Project Gutenberg

The content for this book has been graciously provided by Project Gutenberg. Project Gutenberg is a non-profit organization founded by Michael Hart in 1971 at the University of Illinois. The mission of Project Gutenberg is simple: To encourage the creation and distribution of eBooks. Project Gutenberg is the first and largest collection of public domain eBooks.

A Discourse on the Study of the Law of Nature and Nations

James, Sir Mackintosh

Imprint

This book is part of TREDITION CLASSICS

Author: James, Sir Mackintosh
Cover design: Buchgut, Berlin – Germany

Publisher: tredition GmbH, Hamburg - Germany
ISBN: 978-3-8472-1233-1

www.tredition.com
www.tredition.de

Transcriber's Note

Spelling and punctuation have been preserved as faithfully as possible. Only obvious typographical errors have been corrected.

For ease of reading, the footnotes have been moved to the end of the book.

A DISCOURSE

ON

THE STUDY

OF THE

LAW OF NATURE AND NATIONS.

BY

SIR JAMES MACKINTOSH, M.P.

SECOND EDITION.

LONDON:
HENRY GOODE AND CO.

QUEEN'S HEAD PASSAGE, PATERNOSTER-ROW.

SOLD BY T. CLARK, EDINBURGH; AND WARDLAW AND CO. GLASGOW.

M.DCCC.XXVIII.

A DISCOURSE,

[Page 1]

ETC.

Before I begin a course of lectures on a science of great extent and importance, I think it my duty to lay before the public the reasons which have induced me to undertake such a labour, as well as a short account of the nature and objects of the course which I propose to deliver. I have always been unwilling to waste in unprofitable inactivity that leisure which the first years of my profession usually allow, and which diligent men, even with moderate talents, might often employ in a manner neither discreditable to themselves, nor wholly useless to others. Desirous that my own leisure should not be consumed in sloth, I anxiously looked about for some way of filling it up, which might enable me, according to the measure of my humble abilities, to [Page 2] contribute somewhat to the stock of general usefulness. I had long been convinced that public lectures, which have been used in most ages and countries to teach the elements of almost every part of learning, were the most convenient mode in which these elements could be taught; that they were the best adapted for the important purposes of awakening the attention of the student, of abridging his labours, of guiding his inquiries, of relieving the tediousness of private study, and of impressing on his recollection the principles of science. I saw no reason why the Law of England should be less adapted to this mode of instruction, or less likely to benefit by it, than any other part of knowledge. A learned gentleman, however, had already occupied that ground, [1] and will, I doubt not, persevere in the useful labour which he has undertaken. On his province it was far from my wish to intrude. [Page 3] It appeared to me that a course of lectures on another science closely connected with all liberal professional studies, and which had long been the subject of my own reading and reflection, might not only prove a most useful introduction to the law of England, but might also become an interesting part of general study, and an important branch of the education of those who were not destined for the profession of the law. I was confirmed in my opinion by the assent and approbation of men, whose names, if it were becoming to mention them on so slight an occasion, would add authority to truth, and furnish some excuse even for error. Encouraged by their approbation, I resolved without delay to commence the undertaking, of which I shall now proceed to give some account; without interrupting the progress of my discourse by anticipating or answering the remarks of those who may, perhaps, sneer at me for a departure from the usual course of my profession; because I am desirous of employing in a rational and useful pursuit that leisure, [Page 4] of which the same men would have required no account, if it had been wasted on trifles, or even abused in dissipation.

The science which teaches the rights and duties of men and of states, has, in modern times, been called the Law of Nature and Nations. Under this comprehensive title are included the rules of morality, as they prescribe the conduct of private men towards each other in all the various relations of human life; as they regulate both the obedience of citizens to the laws, and the authority of the magistrate in framing laws and administering government; as they modify the intercourse of independent commonwealths in peace, and prescribe limits to their hostility in war. This important science comprehends only that part of *private ethics* which is capable of being reduced to fixed and general rules. It considers only those general principles of *jurisprudence* and *politics* which the wisdom of the lawgiver adapts to the peculiar situation of his own country, and which the skill of the statesman [Page 5] applies to the more fluctuating and infinitely varying circumstances which affect its immediate welfare and safety. "For there are in nature certain fountains of justice whence all civil laws are derived, but as streams; and like as waters do take tinctures and tastes from the soils through which they run, so do civil laws vary according to the regions and governments where they are planted, though they proceed from the same fountains." [2] —*Bacon's Dig. and Adv. of Learn.* Works, vol. i. p. 101.

On the great questions of morality, of politics, and of municipal law, it is the object of this science to deliver only those fundamental truths of which the particular application is as extensive as the whole private and public conduct of men; to discover those "fountains of justice," without pursuing the "streams" through the endless variety of [Page 6] their course. But another part of the subject is treated with greater fulness and minuteness of application; namely, that important branch of it which professes to regulate the relations and intercourse of states, and more especially, both on account of their greater perfection and their more immediate reference to use, the regulations of that intercourse as they are modified by the usages of the civilised nations of Christendom. Here this science no longer rests in general principles. That province of it which we now call the law of nations, has, in many of its parts, acquired among our European nations much of the precision and certainty of positive law, and the particulars of that law are chiefly to be found in the works of those writers who have treated the science of which I now speak. It is because they have classed (in a manner which seems peculiar to modern times) the duties of individuals with those of nations, and established their obligation on similar grounds, that the whole science has been called, "The Law of Nature and Nations."

Whether this appellation be the happiest that could have been chosen [Page 7] for the science, and by what steps it came to be adopted among our modern moralists and lawyers, [3] are inquiries, perhaps, of more curiosity than use, and which, if they deserve any where to be deeply pursued, will be pursued with more propriety in a full examination of the subject than within the short limits of an introductory discourse. Names are, however, in a great measure arbitrary; but the distribution of knowledge into its parts, though it may often perhaps be varied with [Page 8] little disadvantage, yet certainly depends upon some fixed principles. The modern method of considering individual and national morality as the subjects of the same science, seems to me as convenient and reasonable an arrangement as can be adopted. The same rules of morality which hold together men in families, and which form families into commonwealths, also link together these commonwealths as members of the great society of mankind. Commonwealths, as well as private men, are liable to injury, and capable of benefit, from each other; it is, therefore, their interest as well as their duty to reverence, to practise, and to [Page 9] enforce those rules of justice which control and restrain injury, which regulate and augment benefit, which, even in their present imperfect observance, preserve civilised states in a tolerable condition of security from wrong, and which, if they could be generally obeyed, would establish, and permanently maintain, the well-being of the universal commonwealth of the human race. It is therefore with justice that one part of this science has been called "*the natural law of individuals,*" and the other "*the natural law of states;*" and it is too obvious to require observation, [4] that the application of both these laws, of the former as much as of the latter, is modified and varied by customs, conventions, character, and situation. With a view to these principles, the writers on general jurisprudence have considered states as moral persons; a mode of expression which has been called a fiction of law, [Page 10] but which may be regarded with more propriety as a bold metaphor, used to convey the important truth, that nations, though they acknowledge no common superior, and neither can nor ought to be subjected to human punishment, are yet under the same obligations mutually to practise honesty and humanity, which would have bound individuals, even if they could be conceived ever to have subsisted without the protecting restraints of government; if they were not compelled to the discharge of their duty by the just authority of magistrates, and by the wholesome terrors of the laws. With the same views this law has been styled, and (notwithstanding the objections of some writers to the vagueness of the language) appears to have been styled with great propriety, "the law of nature." It may with sufficient correctness, or at least by an easy metaphor, be called a "*law*," inasmuch as it is a supreme, invariable, and uncontrollable rule of conduct to all men, of which the violation is avenged by natural punishments, which necessarily flow from the [Page 11] constitution of things, and are as fixed and inevitable as the order of nature. It is the "*law of nature*," because its general precepts are essentially adapted to promote the happiness of man, as long as he remains a being of the same nature with which he is at present endowed, or, in other words, as long as he continues to be man, in all the variety of times, places, and circumstances, in which he has been known, or can be imagined to exist; because it is discoverable by natural reason, and suitable to our natural constitution; because its fitness and wisdom are founded on the general nature of human beings, and not on any of those temporary and accidental situations in which they may be placed. It is with still more propriety, and indeed with the highest strictness, and the most perfect accuracy, considered as a law, when, according to those just and magnificent views which philosophy and religion open to us of the government of the world, it is received and reverenced as the sacred code, promulgated by the great Legislator of the Universe for the guidance of his creatures to happiness, guarded and [Page 12] enforced, as our own experience may inform us, by the penal sanctions of shame, of remorse, of infamy, and of misery; and still farther enforced by the reasonable expectation of yet more awful penalties in a future and more permanent state of existence. It is the contemplation of the law of nature under this full, mature, and perfect idea of its high origin and transcendent dignity, that called forth the enthusiasm of the greatest men, and the greatest writers of ancient and modern times, in those sublime descriptions, where they have exhausted all the powers of language, and surpassed all the other exertions, even of their own eloquence, in the display of the beauty and majesty of this sovereign and immutable law. It is of this law that Cicero has spoken in so many parts of his writings, not only with all the splendour and copiousness of eloquence, but with the sensibility of a man of virtue; and with the gravity and comprehension of a philosopher. [5] It is of this law that [Page 13] Hooker speaks in so sublime a strain:—"Of law, no less can be said, than that her seat is the bosom of God, her voice the harmony of the world; all things in heaven and earth do her homage, the very least as feeling her care, the greatest as not exempted from her power; both [Page 14] angels and men, and creatures of what condition soever, though each in different sort and manner, yet all with uniform consent admiring her as the mother of their peace and joy."—*Eccles. Pol.* book i. in the conclusion.

Let not those, who, to use the language of the same Hooker, "talk of truth," without "ever sounding the depth from whence it springeth," hastily take it for granted, that these great masters of eloquence and reason were led astray by the specious delusions of mysticism, from the sober consideration of the true grounds of morality in the nature, necessities, and interests of man. They studied and taught the principles of morals; but they thought it still more necessary, and more wise, a much nobler task, and more becoming a true philosopher, to inspire men with a love and reverence for virtue. [6] They were not [Page 15] contented with elementary speculations. They examined the foundations of our duty, but they felt and cherished a most natural, a most seemly, a most rational enthusiasm, when they contemplated the majestic edifice which is reared on these solid foundations. They devoted the highest exertions of their mind to spread that beneficent enthusiasm among men. They consecrated as a homage to virtue the most perfect fruits of their genius. If these grand sentiments of "the good and fair" have sometimes prevented them from delivering the principles of ethics with the nakedness and dryness of science, at least, we must own that they have chosen the better part; that they have preferred virtuous feeling to moral theory; and practical benefit to speculative exactness. Perhaps these wise men may have supposed that the minute dissection and anatomy of Virtue might, to the ill-judging eye, weaken the charm of her [Page 16] beauty.

It is not for me to attempt a theme which has perhaps been exhausted by these great writers. I am indeed much less called upon to display the worth and usefulness of the law of nations, than to vindicate myself from presumption in attempting a subject which has been already handled by so many masters. For the purpose of that vindication it will be necessary to sketch a very short and slight account (for such in this place it must unavoidably be) of the progress and present state of the science, and of that succession of able writers who have gradually brought it to its present perfection.

We have no Greek or Roman treatise remaining on the law of nations. From the title of one of the lost works of Aristotle, it appears that he composed a treatise on the laws of war, [7] which, if we had the good fortune to possess it, would doubtless have amply satisfied our curiosity, and would have taught us both the practice of the ancient nations and the opinions of their moralists, with that depth and [Page 17] precision which distinguish the other works of that great philosopher. We can now only imperfectly collect that practice and those opinions from various passages which are scattered over the writings of philosophers, historians, poets, and orators. When the time shall arrive for a more full consideration of the state of the government and manners of the ancient world, I shall be able, perhaps, to offer satisfactory reasons why these enlightened nations did not separate from the general province of ethics that part of morality which regulates the intercourse of states, and erect it into an independent science. It would require a long discussion to unfold the various causes which united the modern nations of Europe into a closer society; which linked them together by the firmest bands of mutual dependence, and which thus, in process of time, gave to the law that regulated their intercourse greater importance, higher improvement, and more binding force. Among these causes we may enumerate a common extraction, a common religion, similar manners, institutions, and languages; in earlier ages the authority of [Page 18] the See of Rome, and the extravagant claims of the imperial crown; in later times the connexions of trade, the jealousy of power, the refinement of civilization, the cultivation of science, and, above all, that general mildness of character and manners which arose from the combined and progressive influence of chivalry, of commerce, of learning, and of religion. Nor must we omit the similarity of those political institutions which, in every country that had been over-run by the Gothic conquerors, bore discernible marks (which the revolutions of succeeding ages had obscured, but not obliterated) of the rude but bold and noble outline of liberty that was originally sketched by the hand of these generous barbarians. These and many other causes conspired to unite the nations of Europe in a more intimate connexion and a more constant intercourse, and of consequence made the regulation of their intercourse more necessary, and the law that was to govern it more important. In proportion as they approached to the condition of [Page 19] provinces of the same empire, it became almost as essential that Europe should have a precise and comprehensive code of the law of nations, as that each country should have a system of municipal law. The labours of the learned accordingly began to be directed to this subject in the sixteenth century, soon after the revival of learning, and after that regular distribution of power and territory which has subsisted, with little variation, until our times. The critical examination of these early writers would perhaps not be very interesting in an extensive work, and it would be unpardonable in a short discourse. It is sufficient to observe that they were all more or less shackled by the barbarous philosophy of the schools, and that they were impeded in their progress by a timorous deference for the inferior and technical parts of [Page 20] the Roman law, without raising their views to the comprehensive principles which will for ever inspire mankind with veneration for that grand monument of human wisdom. It was only indeed in the sixteenth century that the Roman law was first studied and understood as a science connected with Roman history and literature, and illustrated by men whom Ulpian and Papinian would not have disdained to acknowledge as their successors. [8] Among the writers of that age we may perceive the ineffectual attempts, the partial advances, the occasional streaks of light which always precede great discoveries, and works that are to instruct posterity.

The reduction of the law of nations to a system was reserved for Grotius. It was by the advice of Lord Bacon and Peiresc that he undertook this arduous task. He produced a work which we now indeed justly deem imperfect, but which is perhaps the most complete that the world has yet owed, at so early a stage in the progress of any science, [Page 21] to the genius and learning of one man. So great is the uncertainty of posthumous reputation, and so liable is the fame even of the greatest men to be obscured by those new fashions of thinking and writing which succeed each other so rapidly among polished nations, that Grotius, who filled so large a space in the eye of his contemporaries, is now perhaps known to some of my readers only by name. Yet if we fairly estimate both his endowments and his virtues, we may justly consider him as one of the most memorable men who have done honour to modern times. He combined the discharge of the most important duties of active and public life with the attainment of that exact and various learning which is generally the portion only of the recluse student. He was distinguished as an advocate and a magistrate, and he composed the most valuable works on the law of his own country; he was almost equally celebrated as an historian, a scholar, a poet, and a divine; a disinterested statesman, a philosophical lawyer, a patriot who united moderation with firmness, and a theologian who was taught candour by his learning. Unmerited exile did not damp his patriotism; the bitterness of controversy did not [Page 22] extinguish his charity. The sagacity of his numerous and fierce adversaries could not discover a blot on his character; and in the midst of all the hard trials and galling provocations of a turbulent political life, he never once deserted his friends when they were unfortunate, nor insulted his enemies when they were weak. In times of the most furious civil and religious faction he preserved his name unspotted, and he knew how to reconcile fidelity to his own party, with moderation towards his opponents. Such was the man who was destined to give a new form to the law of nations, or rather to create a science, of which only rude sketches and indigested materials were scattered over the writings of those who had gone before him. By tracing the laws of his country to their principles, he was led to the contemplation of the law of nature, which be justly considered as the parent of all municipal law. [9] Few works were more celebrated than that of Grotius in his own days, and in [Page 23] the age which succeeded. It has, however, been the fashion of the last half-century to depreciate his work as a shapeless compilation, in which reason lies buried under a mass of authorities and quotations. This fashion originated among French wits and declaimers, and it has been, I know not for what reason, adopted, though with far greater moderation and decency, by some respectable writers among ourselves. As to those who first used this language, the most candid supposition that we can make with respect to them is, that they never read the work; for, if they had not been deterred from the perusal of it by such a formidable display of Greek characters, they must soon have discovered that Grotius never quotes on any subject till he has first appealed to some principles, and often, in my humble opinion, though, not always, to the soundest and most rational principles.

But another sort of answer is due to some of those [10] who have criticised Grotius, [Page 24] and that answer might be given in the words of Grotius himself. [11] He was not of such a stupid and servile cast of mind, as to quote the opinions of poets or orators, of historians and philosophers, as those of judges, from whose decision there was no appeal. He quotes them, as he tells us himself, as witnesses whose conspiring testimony, mightily strengthened and confirmed by their discordance on almost every other subject, is a conclusive proof of the unanimity of the whole human race on the great rules of duty and the fundamental principles of morals. On such matters, poets and orators are the most unexceptionable of all witnesses; for they address themselves to the general feelings and sympathies of mankind; they are neither warped by system, nor perverted by sophistry; they can attain none of their objects; they can neither please nor persuade if they dwell on moral sentiments not in unison with those of their readers. No system of moral philosophy can surely disregard the general feelings of [Page 25] human nature and the according judgment of all ages and nations. But where are these feelings and that judgment recorded and preserved? In those very writings which Grotius is gravely blamed for having quoted. The usages and laws of nations, the events of history, the opinions of philosophers, the sentiments of orators and poets, as well as the observation of common life, are, in truth, the materials out of which the science of morality is formed; and those who neglect them are justly chargeable with a vain attempt to philosophise without regard to fact and experience, the sole foundation of all true philosophy.

If this were merely an objection of taste, I should be willing to allow that Grotius has indeed poured forth his learning with a profusion that sometimes rather encumbers than adorns his work, and which is not always necessary to the illustration of his subject. Yet, even in making that concession, I should rather yield to the taste of others than speak from my own feelings. I own that such richness and splendour of literature have a powerful [Page 26] charm for me. They fill my mind with an endless variety of delightful recollections and associations. They relieve the understanding in its progress through a vast science, by calling up the memory of great men and of interesting events. By this means we see the truths of morality clothed with all the eloquence (not that could be produced by the powers of one man, but) that could be bestowed on them by the collective genius of the world. Even Virtue and Wisdom themselves acquire new majesty in my eyes, when I thus see all the great masters of thinking and writing called together, as it were, from all times and countries, to do them homage, and to appear in their train.

But this is no place for discussions of taste, and I am very ready to own that mine may be corrupted. The work of Grotius is liable to a more serious objection, though I do not recollect that it has ever been made. His method is inconvenient and unscientific. He has inverted the natural order. That natural order undoubtedly dictates, that we should first search for the original principles of the science [Page 27] in human nature; then apply them to the regulation of the conduct of individuals, and lastly, employ them for the decision of those difficult and complicated questions that arise with respect to the intercourse of nations. But Grotius has chosen the reverse of this method. He begins with the consideration of the states of peace and war, and he examines original principles only occasionally and incidentally as they grow out of the questions which he is called upon to decide. It is a necessary consequence of this disorderly method, which exhibits the elements of the science in the form of scattered digressions, that he seldom employs sufficient discussion on these fundamental truths, and never in the place where such a discussion would be most instructive to the reader.

This defect in the plan of Grotius was perceived, and supplied, by Puffendorff, who restored natural law to that superiority which belonged to it, and with great propriety treated the law of nations as only one main branch of the parent stock. Without the genius of his master, and with very inferior [Page 28] learning, he has yet treated this subject with sound sense, with clear method, with extensive and accurate knowledge, and with a copiousness of detail sometimes indeed tedious, but always instructive and satisfactory. His work will be always studied by those who spare no labour to acquire a deep knowledge of the subject; but it will, in our times, I fear, be oftener found on the shelf than on the desk of the general student. In the time of Mr. Locke it was considered as the manual of those who were intended for active life; but in the present age I believe it will be found that men of business are too much occupied, men of letters are too fastidious, and men of the world too indolent, for the study or even the perusal of such works. Far be it from me to derogate from the real and great merit of so useful a writer as Puffendorff. His treatise is a mine in which all his successors must dig. I only presume to suggest, that a book so prolix, and so utterly void of all the attractions of composition, is likely to repel many readers who are interested, and who might perhaps be disposed to acquire [Page 29] some knowledge of the principles of public law.

Many other circumstances might be mentioned, which conspire to prove that neither of the great works of which I have spoken, has superseded the necessity of a new attempt to lay before the public a System of the Law of Nations. The language of science is so completely changed since both these works were written, that whoever was now to employ their terms in his moral reasonings would be almost unintelligible to some of his hearers or readers; and to some among them too who are neither ill qualified nor ill disposed to study such subjects with considerable advantage to themselves. The learned indeed well know how little novelty or variety is to be found in scientific disputes. The same truths and the same errors have been repeated from age to age, with little variation but in the language; and novelty of expression is often mistaken by the ignorant for substantial discovery. Perhaps too very nearly the same portion of genius and judgment has been exerted in most of the various forms under which science [Page 30] has been cultivated at different periods of history. The superiority of those writers who continue to be read, perhaps often consists chiefly in taste, in prudence, in a happy choice of subject, in a favourable moment, in an agreeable style, in the good fortune of a prevalent language, or in other advantages which are either accidental, or are the result rather of the secondary than of the highest faculties of the mind.—But these reflections, while they moderate the pride of invention, and dispel the extravagant conceit of superior illumination, yet serve to prove the use, and indeed the necessity, of composing, from time to time, new systems of science adapted to the opinions and language of each succeeding period. Every age must be taught in its own language. If a man were now to begin a discourse on ethics with an account of the "*moral entities*" of Puffendorff, [12] he would speak an unknown tongue. [Page 31]

It is not, however, alone as a mere translation of former writers into modern language that a new system of public law seems likely to be useful. The age in which we live possesses many advantages which are peculiarly favourable to such an undertaking. Since the composition of the great works of Grotius and Puffendorff, a more modest, simple, and intelligible philosophy has been introduced into the schools; which has indeed been grossly abused by sophists, but which, from the time of Locke, has been cultivated and improved by a succession of disciples worthy of their illustrious master. We are thus enabled to discuss with precision, and to explain with clearness, the principles of the science of human nature, which are in themselves on a level with the capacity of every man of good sense, and which only appeared to be abstruse from [Page 32] the unprofitable subtleties with which they were loaded, and the barbarous jargon in which they were expressed. The deepest doctrines of morality have since that time been treated in the perspicuous and popular style, and with some degree of the beauty and eloquence of the ancient moralists. That philosophy on which are founded the principles of our duty, if it has not become more certain (for morality admits no discoveries), is at least less "harsh and crabbed," less obscure and haughty in its language, less forbidding and disgusting in its appearance, than in the days of our ancestors. If this progress of learning towards popularity has engendered (as it must be owned that it has) a multitude of superficial and most mischievous sciolists, the antidote must come from the same quarter with the disease. Popular reason can alone correct popular sophistry.

Nor is this the only advantage which a writer of the present age would possess over the celebrated jurists of the last century. Since that time vast additions have been [Page 33] made to the stock of our knowledge of human nature. Many dark periods of history have since been explored. Many hitherto unknown regions of the globe have been visited and described by travellers and navigators not less intelligent than intrepid. We may be said to stand at the confluence of the greatest number of streams of knowledge flowing from the most distant sources that ever met at one point. We are not confined, as the learned of the last age generally were, to the history of those renowned nations who are our masters in literature. We can bring before us man in a lower and more abject condition than any in which he was ever before seen. The records have been partly opened to us of those mighty empires of Asia [13] where the [Page 34] beginnings of civilization are lost in the darkness of an unfathomable antiquity. We can make human society pass in review before our mind, from the brutal and helpless barbarism of *Terra del Fuego*, and the mild and voluptuous savages of Otaheite, to the tame, but ancient and immovable civilization of China, which bestows its own arts on every successive race of conquerors; to the meek and servile natives of Hindostan, who preserve their ingenuity, their skill, and their science, through a long series of ages, under the yoke of foreign tyrants; to the gross and incorrigible rudeness of the Ottomans, incapable of improvement, and extinguishing the remains of civilization among their unhappy subjects, once the most ingenious nations of the earth. We can examine almost every imaginable variety in [Page 35] the character, manners, opinions, feelings, prejudices, and institutions of mankind, into which they can be thrown, either by the rudeness of barbarism, or by the capricious corruptions of refinement, or by those innumerable combinations of circumstances, which, both in these opposite conditions and in all the intermediate stages between them, influence or direct the course of human affairs. History, if I may be allowed the expression, is now a vast museum, in which specimens of every variety of human nature may be studied. From these great accessions to knowledge, law-givers and statesmen, but, above all, moralists and political philosophers, may reap the most important instruction. They may plainly discover in all the useful and beautiful variety of governments and institutions, and under all the fantastic multitude of usages and rites which have prevailed among men, the same fundamental, comprehensive truths, the sacred master-principles which are the guardians of human society, recognised and revered (with few and slight exceptions) by every nation upon earth, and uniformly taught (with still [Page 36] fewer exceptions) by a succession of wise men from the first dawn of speculation to the present moment. The exceptions, few as they are, will, on more reflection, be found rather apparent than real. If we could raise ourselves to that height from which we ought to survey so vast a subject, these exceptions would altogether vanish; the brutality of a handful of savages would disappear in the immense prospect of human nature, and the murmurs of a few licentious sophists would not ascend to break the general harmony. This consent of mankind in first principles, and this endless variety in their application, which is one among many valuable truths which we may collect from our present extensive acquaintance with the history of man, is itself of vast importance. Much of the majesty and authority of virtue is derived from their consent, and almost the whole of practical wisdom is founded on their variety.

What former age could have supplied facts for such a work as that of Montesquieu? He indeed has been, perhaps justly, charged with abusing this advantage, by the undistinguishing [Page 37] adoption of the narratives of travellers of very different degrees of accuracy and veracity. But if we reluctantly confess the justness of this objection; if we are compelled to own that he exaggerates the influence of climate, that he ascribes too much to the foresight and forming skill of legislators, and far too little to time and circumstances, in the growth of political constitutions; that the substantial character and essential differences of governments are often lost and confounded in his technical language and arrangement; that he often bends the free and irregular outline of nature to the imposing but fallacious geometrical regularity of system; that he has chosen a style of affected abruptness, sententiousness, and vivacity, ill suited to the gravity of his subject: after all these concessions (for his fame is large enough to spare many concessions), the Spirit of Laws will still remain not only one of the most solid and durable monuments of the powers of the human mind, but a striking evidence of the inestimable advantages which political philosophy may receive from a wide survey of [Page 38] all the various conditions of human society.

In the present century a slow and silent, but very substantial mitigation has taken place in the practice of war; and in proportion as that mitigated practice has received the sanction of time, it is raised from the rank of mere usage, and becomes part of the law of nations. Whoever will compare our present modes of warfare with the system of Grotius [14] will clearly discern the immense improvements which have taken place in that respect since the publication of his work, during a period, perhaps in every point of view, the happiest to be found in the history of the world. In the same period many important points of public law have been the subject of contest both by argument and by arms, of which we find either no mention, or very obscure traces, in the history of preceding times.

There are other circumstances to which I [Page 39] allude with hesitation and reluctance, though it must be owned that they afford to a writer of this age some degree of unfortunate and deplorable advantage over his predecessors. Recent events have accumulated more terrible practical instruction on every subject of politics than could have been in other times acquired by the experience of ages. Men's wit, sharpened by their passions, has penetrated to the bottom of almost all political questions. Even the fundamental rules of morality themselves have, for the first time, unfortunately for mankind, become the subject of doubt and discussion. I shall consider it as my duty to abstain from all mention of these awful events, and of these fatal controversies. But the mind of that man must indeed be incurious and indocile, who has either overlooked all these things; or reaped no instruction from the contemplation of them.

From these reflections it appears, that, since the composition of those two great works on the Law of Nature and Nations which continue to be the classical and standard works [Page 40] on that subject, we have gained both more convenient instruments of reasoning and more extensive materials for science; that the code of war has been enlarged and improved; that new questions have been practically decided; and that new controversies have arisen regarding the intercourse of independent states, and the first principles of morality and civil government.

Some readers may, however, think that in these observations which I offer, to excuse the presumption of my own attempt, I have omitted the mention of later writers, to whom some part of the remarks is not justly applicable. But, perhaps, further consideration will acquit me in the judgment of such readers. Writers on particular questions of public law are not within the scope of my observations. They have furnished the most valuable materials; but I speak only of a system. To the large work of Wolffius, the observations which I have made on Puffendorff as a book for general use, will surely apply with tenfold force. His abridger, Vattel, deserves, indeed, considerable praise. He is a [Page 41] very ingenious, clear, elegant, and useful writer. But he only considers one part of this extensive subject, namely, the law of nations strictly so called; and I cannot help thinking, that, even in this department of the science, he has adopted some doubtful and dangerous principles, not to mention his constant deficiency in that fulness of example and illustration, which so much embellishes and strengthens reason. It is hardly necessary to take any notice of the text-book of Heineccius, the best writer of elementary books with whom I am acquainted on any subject. Burlamaqui is an author of superior merit; but he confines himself too much to the general principles of morality and politics, to require much observation from me in this place. The same reason will excuse me for passing over in silence the works of many philosophers and moralists, to whom, in the course of my proposed lectures, I shall owe and confess the greatest obligations; and it might perhaps deliver me from the necessity of speaking of the work of Dr. Paley, if I were not desirous of this public opportunity of professing [Page 42] my gratitude for the instruction and pleasure which I have received from that excellent writer, who possesses, in so eminent a degree, those invaluable qualities of a moralist, good sense, caution, sobriety, and perpetual reference to convenience and practice; and who certainly is thought less original than he really is, merely because his taste and modesty have led him to disdain the ostentation of novelty, and because he generally employs more art to blend his own arguments with the body of received opinions, so as that they are scarce to be distinguished, than other men, in the pursuit of a transient popularity, have exerted to disguise the most miserable common-places in the shape of paradox.

No writer since the time of Grotius, of Puffendorff, and of Wolf, has combined an investigation of the principles of natural and public law, with a full application of these principles to particular cases; and in these circumstances, I trust, it will not be deemed extravagant presumption in me to hope that I shall be able to exhibit a view of this science, which shall, at least, be more intelligible and [Page 43] attractive to students, than the learned treatises of these celebrated men. I shall now proceed to state the general plan and subjects of the lectures in which I am to make this attempt.

I. The being whose actions the law of nature professes to regulate, is man. It is on the knowledge of his nature that the science of his duty must be founded. [15] It is impossible to approach the threshold of moral philosophy, without a previous examination of the faculties and habits of the human mind. Let no reader be repelled from this examination, by the odious and terrible name of *metaphysics;* for it is, in truth, nothing more than the employment of good sense, in observing our own thoughts, feelings, and actions; and when the facts which are thus observed, are expressed as they ought to be, in plain language, it is, perhaps, above all other sciences, most on a level with the capacity and information [Page 44] of the generality of thinking men. When it is thus expressed, it requires no previous qualification, but a sound judgment, perfectly to comprehend it; and those who wrap it up in a technical and mysterious jargon, always give us strong reason to suspect that they are not philosophers but impostors. Whoever thoroughly understands such a science, must be able to teach it plainly to all men of common sense. The proposed course will therefore open with a very short, and, I hope, a very simple and intelligible account of the powers and operations of the human mind. By this plain statement of facts, it will not be difficult to decide many celebrated, though frivolous, and merely verbal controversies, which have long amused the leisure of the schools, and which owe both their fame and their existence to the ambiguous obscurity of scholastic language. It will, for example, only require an appeal to every man's experience, to prove that we often act purely from a regard to the happiness of others, and are therefore social beings; and it is not necessary to be a consummate

[Page 45] judge of the deceptions of language, to despise the sophistical trifler, who tells us, that, because we experience a gratification in our benevolent actions, we are therefore exclusively and uniformly selfish. A correct examination of facts will lead us to discover that quality which is common to all virtuous actions, and which distinguishes them from those which are vicious and criminal. But we shall see that it is necessary for man to be governed not by his own transient and hasty opinion upon the tendency of every particular action, but by those fixed and unalterable rules, which are the joint result of the impartial judgment, the natural feelings, and the embodied experience of mankind. The authority of these rules is, indeed, founded only on their tendency to promote private and public welfare; but the morality of actions will appear solely to consist in their correspondence with the rule. By the help of this obvious distinction we shall vindicate a just theory, which, far from being modern, is, in fact, as ancient as philosophy, both from plausible objections, and from the odious [Page 46] imputation of supporting those absurd and monstrous systems which have been built upon it. Beneficial tendency is the foundation of rules, and the criterion by which habits and sentiments are to be tried. But it is neither the immediate standard, nor can it ever be the principal motive of action. An action, to be completely virtuous, must accord with moral rules, and must flow from our natural feelings and affections, moderated, matured, and improved into steady habits of right conduct. [16] Without, however, dwelling longer on subjects which cannot be clearly stated, unless they are fully unfolded, I content myself with observing, that it shall be my object, in this preliminary, but most important part of the course, to lay the foundations of morality so deeply in human nature, as may satisfy the coldest inquirer; and, at the same time, to vindicate the paramount authority of the rules of our duty, at all times, [Page 47] and in all places, over all opinions of interest and speculations of benefit, so extensively, so universally, and so inviolably, as may well justify the grandest and the most apparently extravagant effusions of moral enthusiasm. If, notwithstanding all my endeavours to deliver these doctrines with the utmost simplicity, any of my auditors should still reproach me for introducing such abstruse matters, I must shelter myself behind the authority of the wisest of men. "If they (the ancient moralists), before they had come to the popular and received notions of virtue and vice, had staid a little longer upon the inquiry concerning *the roots of good and evil,* they had given, in my opinion, a great light to that which followed; and specially if they had consulted with nature, they had made their doctrines less prolix, and more profound."—*Bacon. Dign. and Adv. of Learn.* book ii. What Lord Bacon desired for the mere gratification of scientific curiosity, the welfare of mankind now imperiously demands. Shallow systems of metaphysics have given birth to a brood of abominable and pestilential [Page 48] paradoxes, which nothing but a more profound philosophy can destroy. However we may, perhaps, lament the necessity of discussions which may shake the habitual reverence of some men for those rules which it is the chief interest of all men to practise, we have now no choice left. We must either dispute, or abandon the ground. Undistinguishing and unmerited invectives against philosophy, will only harden sophists and their disciples in the insolent conceit, that they are in possession of an undisputed superiority of reason; and that their antagonists have no arms to employ against them, but those of popular declamation. Let us not for a moment even appear to suppose, that philosophical truth and human happiness are so irreconcilably at variance. I cannot express my opinion on this subject so well as in the words of a most valuable, though generally neglected writer: "The science of abstruse learning, when completely attained, is like Achilles's spear, that healed the wounds it had made before; so this knowledge serves to repair the damage itself had occasioned, and this perhaps is all it [Page 49] is good for; it casts no additional light upon the paths of life, but disperses the clouds with which it had overspread them before; it advances not the traveller one step in his journey, but conducts him back again to the spot from whence he wandered. Thus the land of Philosophy consists partly of an open champaign country, passable by every common understanding, and partly of a range of woods, traversable only by the speculative, and where they too frequently delight to amuse themselves. Since then we shall be obliged to make incursions into this latter tract, and shall probably find it a region of obscurity, danger, and difficulty, it behoves us to use our utmost endeavours for enlightening and smoothing the way before us." [17] We shall, however, remain in the forest only long enough to visit the fountains of those streams which flow from it, and which water and fertilise the cultivated region of Morals, to become acquainted with the modes of warfare practised by its savage [Page 50] inhabitants, and to learn the means of guarding our fair and fruitful land against their desolating incursions. I shall hasten from speculations, to which I am naturally, perhaps, but too prone, and proceed to the more profitable consideration of our practical duty.

II. The first and most simple part of ethics is that which regards the duties of private men towards each other, when they are considered apart from the sanction of positive laws. I say, *apart* from that sanction, not *antecedent* to it; for though we *separate* private from political duties for the sake of greater clearness and order in reasoning, yet we are not to be so deluded by this mere arrangement of convenience as to suppose that human society ever has subsisted, or ever could subsist, without being protected by government and bound together by laws. All these relative duties of private life have been so copiously and beautifully treated by the moralists of antiquity, that few men will now choose to follow them who are not actuated by the wild ambition of equalling Aristotle in precision, or rivalling Cicero in eloquence. [Page 51] They have been also admirably treated by modern moralists, among whom it would be gross injustice not to number many of the preachers of the Christian religion, whose peculiar character is that spirit of universal charity, which is the living principle of all our social duties. For it was long ago said, with great truth, by Lord Bacon, "that there never was any philosophy, religion, or other discipline, which did so plainly and highly exalt that good which is communicative, and depress the good which is private and particular, as the Christian faith." [18] The appropriate praise of this religion is not so much, that it has taught new duties, as that it breathes a milder and more benevolent spirit over the whole extent of morals.

On a subject which has been so exhausted, I should naturally have contented myself with the most slight and general survey, if some fundamental principles had not of late been brought into question, which, in all former times, have been deemed too evident to [Page 52] require the support of argument, and almost too sacred to admit the liberty of discussion. I shall here endeavour to strengthen some parts of the fortifications of morality which have hitherto been neglected, because no man had ever been hardy enough to attack them. Almost all the relative duties of human life will be found more immediately, or more remotely, to arise out of the two great institutions of property and marriage. They constitute, preserve, and improve society. Upon their gradual improvement depends the progressive civilization of mankind; on them rests the whole order of civil life. We are told by Horace, that the first efforts of lawgivers to civilise men consisted in strengthening and regulating these institutions, and fencing them round with rigorous penal laws.

Oppida cœperunt munire et ponere leges
Neu quis fur esset, neu quis latro, neu quis adulter.
1 *Serm.* iii. 105.

A celebrated ancient orator, of whose poems we have but a few fragments remaining, has well described the progressive order in which [Page 53] human society is gradually led to its highest improvements under the guardianship of those laws which secure property and regulate marriage.

Et leges sanctas docuit, et chara jugavit
Corpora conjugiis; et magnas condidit urbes.

Frag. C. Licin. Calvi.

These two great institutions convert the selfish as well as the social passions of our nature into the firmest bands of a peaceable and orderly intercourse; they change the sources of discord into principles of quiet; they discipline the most ungovernable, they refine the grossest, and they exalt the most sordid propensities; so that they become the perpetual fountain of all that strengthens, and preserves, and adorns society; they sustain the individual, and they perpetuate the race. Around these institutions all our social duties will be found at various distances to range themselves; some more near, obviously essential to the good order of human life, others more remote, and of which the necessity is not at first view so apparent; and some so distant, that [Page 54] their importance has been sometimes doubted, though upon more mature consideration they will be found to be outposts and advanced guards of these fundamental principles: that man should securely enjoy the fruits of his labour, and that the society of the sexes should be so wisely ordered as to make it a school of the kind affections, and a fit nursery for the commonwealth.

The subject of *property* is of great extent. It will be necessary to establish the foundation of the rights of acquisition, alienation, and transmission, not in imaginary contracts or a pretended state of nature, but in their subserviency to the subsistence and well-being of mankind. It will not only be curious, but useful, to trace the history of property from the first loose and transient occupancy of the savage, through all the modifications which it has at different times received, to that comprehensive, subtle, and anxiously minute code of property which is the last result of the most refined civilization.

I shall observe the same order in considering the society of the sexes as it is regulated [Page 55] by the institution of marriage. [19] I shall endeavour to lay open those unalterable principles of general interest on which that institution rests: and if I entertain a hope that on this subject I may be able to add something to what our masters in morality have taught us, I trust, that the reader will bear in mind, as an excuse for my presumption, that *they* were not likely to employ much argument where they did not foresee the possibility of doubt. I shall also consider the history [20] of marriage, and trace it through [Page 56] all the forms which it has assumed, to that decent and happy permanency of union, which has, perhaps above all other causes, contributed to the quiet of society, and the refinement of manners in modern times. Among many other inquiries which this subject will suggest, I shall be led more particularly to examine the natural station and duties of the female sex, their condition among different nations, its improvement in Europe, and the bounds which Nature herself has prescribed to the progress of that improvement; beyond which, every pretended advance will be a real degradation.

III. Having established the principles of private duty, I shall proceed to consider [Page 57] man under the important relation of subject and sovereign, or, in other words, of citizen and magistrate. The duties which arise from this relation I shall endeavour to establish, not upon supposed compacts, which are altogether chimerical, which must be admitted to be false in fact, which if they are to be considered as fictions, will be found to serve no purpose of just reasoning, and to be equally the foundation of a system of universal despotism in Hobbes, and of universal anarchy in Rousseau; but on the solid basis of general convenience. Men cannot subsist without society and mutual aid; they can neither maintain social intercourse nor receive aid from each other without the protection of government; and they cannot enjoy that protection without submitting to the restraints which a just government imposes. This plain argument establishes the duty of obedience on the part of citizens, and the duty of protection on that of magistrates, on the same foundation with that of every other moral duty; and it shews, with sufficient evidence, that these duties are reciprocal; the only rational end for which the [Page 58] fiction of a contract could have been invented. I shall not encumber my reasoning by any speculations on the origin of government; a question on which so much reason has been wasted in modern times; but which the ancients [21] in a higher spirit of philosophy have never once mooted. If our principles be just, the origin of government must have been coeval with that of mankind; and as no tribe has ever yet been discovered so brutish as to be without some government, and yet so enlightened as to establish a government by common consent, it is surely unnecessary to employ any serious argument in the confutation of a doctrine that is inconsistent with [Page 59] reason, and unsupported by experience. But though all inquiries into the origin of government be chimerical, yet the history of its progress is curious and useful. The various stages through which it passed from savage independence, which implies every man's power of injuring his neighbour, to legal liberty, which consists in every man's security against wrong; the manner in which a family expands into a tribe, and tribes coalesce into a nation; in which public justice is gradually engrafted on private revenge, find temporary submission ripened into habitual obedience; form a most important and extensive subject of inquiry, which comprehends all the improvements of mankind in police, in judicature, and in legislation.

I have already given the reader to understand that the description of liberty which seems to me the most comprehensive, is that of *security against wrong*. Liberty is therefore the object of all government. Men are more free under every government, even the most imperfect, than they would be if it were possible for them to exist without any government [Page 60] at all: they are more secure from wrong, *more undisturbed in the exercise of their natural powers, and therefore more free, even in the most obvious and grossest sense of the word*, than if they were altogether unprotected against injury from each other. But as general security is enjoyed in very different degrees under different governments, those which guard it most perfectly, are by way of eminence called *free*. Such governments attain most completely the end which is common to all government. A free constitution of government and a good constitution of government are therefore different expressions for the same idea.

Another material distinction, however, soon presents itself. In most civilised states the subject is tolerably protected against gross injustice from his fellows by impartial laws, which it is the manifest interest of the sovereign to enforce. But some commonwealths are so happy as to be founded on a principle of much more refined and provident wisdom. The subjects of such commonwealths are guarded not only against the injustice of each [Page 61] other, but (as far as human prudence can contrive) against oppression from the magistrate. Such states, like all other extraordinary examples of public or private excellence and happiness, are thinly scattered over the different ages and countries of the world. In them the will of the sovereign is limited with so exact a measure, that his protecting authority is not weakened. Such a combination of skill and fortune is not often to be expected, and indeed never can arise, but from the constant though gradual exertions of wisdom and virtue, to improve a long succession of most favourable circumstances.

There is indeed scarce any society so wretched as to be destitute of some sort of weak provision against the injustice of their governors. Religious institutions, favourite prejudices, national manners, have in different countries, with unequal degrees of force, checked or mitigated the exercise of supreme power. The privileges of a powerful nobility, of opulent mercantile communities, of great judicial corporations, have in some monarchies approached more near to a control on the [Page 62] sovereign. Means have been devised with more or less wisdom to temper the despotism of an aristocracy over their subjects, and in democracies to protect the minority against the majority, and the whole people against the tyranny of demagogues. But in these unmixed forms of government, as the right of legislation is vested in one individual or in one order, it is obvious that the legislative power may shake off all the restraints which the laws have imposed on it. All such governments, therefore, tend towards despotism, and the securities which they admit against mis-government are extremely feeble and precarious. The best security which human wisdom can devise, seems to be the distribution of political authority among different individuals and bodies, with separate interests and separate characters, corresponding to the variety of classes of which civil society is composed, each interested to guard their own order from oppression by the rest; each also interested to prevent any of the others from seizing on exclusive, and therefore despotic power; and all having a common interest to [Page 63] co-operate in carrying on the ordinary and necessary administration of government. If there were not an interest to resist each other in extraordinary cases, there would not be liberty. If there were not an interest to co-operate in the ordinary course of affairs, there could be no government. The object of such wise institutions which make the selfishness of governors a security against their injustice, is to protect men against wrong both from their rulers and their fellows. Such governments are, with justice, peculiarly and emphatically called *free*; and in ascribing that liberty to the skilful combination of mutual dependence and mutual check, I feel my own conviction greatly strengthened by calling to mind, that in this opinion I agree with all the wise men who have ever deeply considered the principles of politics; with Aristotle and Polybius, with Cicero and Tacitus, with Bacon and Machiavel, with Montesquieu and Hume. [22] It is [Page 64] impossible in such a cursory sketch as the present, even to allude to a very small part of those philosophical principles, political reasonings, and historical facts, which are necessary for the illustration of this momentous subject. In a full discussion of it I shall be [Page 65] obliged to examine the general frame of the most celebrated governments of ancient and modern times, and especially of those which have been most renowned for their freedom. The result of such an examination will be, that no institution so detestable as an absolutely unbalanced government, perhaps ever existed; that the simple governments are mere creatures of the imagination of theorists, who have transformed names used for the convenience of arrangement into real polities; that, as constitutions of government approach more nearly to that unmixed and uncontrolled simplicity they become despotic, and as they recede farther from that simplicity they become free.

By the constitution of a state, I mean "*the body of those written and unwritten fundamental laws which regulate the most important rights of the higher magistrates, and the most essential privileges* [23] *of the subjects.*" [Page 66] Such a body of political laws must in all countries arise out of the character and situation of a people; they must grow with its progress, be adapted to its peculiarities, change with its changes; and be incorporated into its habits. Human wisdom cannot form such a constitution by one act, for human wisdom cannot create the materials of which it is composed. The attempt, always ineffectual, to change by violence the ancient habits of men, and the established order of society, so as to fit them for an absolutely new scheme of government, flows from the most presumptuous ignorance, requires the support of the most ferocious tyranny, and leads to consequences which its authors can never foresee; generally, indeed, to institutions the most opposite to those of which they profess to seek the [Page 67] establishment. [24] But human wisdom indefatigably employed for remedying abuses, and in seizing favourable opportunities of improving that order of society which arises from causes over which we have little control, after the reforms and amendments of a series of ages, has sometimes, though very rarely, [25] shewn itself capable of building up a free constitution, which [Page 68] is "the growth of time and nature, rather than the work of human invention." Such a constitution can only be formed by the wise imitation of "*the great innovator* Time, which, indeed, innovateth greatly, but quietly, and by degrees scarce to be perceived." [26] Without descending to the puerile ostentation of panegyric, on that of which all mankind confess the excellence, I may observe, with truth and soberness, that a free government not only establishes an universal security against wrong, but that it also cherishes all the noblest powers of the human mind; that it tends to banish both the mean and the ferocious vices; that it improves the national character to which it is adapted, and out of which it grows; that its whole administration is a practical school of honesty and humanity; and that there the social affections, expanded into public spirit, gain a wider sphere, and a more active spring.

I shall conclude what I have to offer on government, by an account of the constitution [Page 69] of England. I shall endeavour to trace the progress of that constitution by the light of history, of laws, and of records, from the earliest times to the present age; and to shew how the general principles of liberty, originally common to it, with the other Gothic monarchies of Europe, but in other countries lost or obscured, were in this more fortunate island preserved, matured, and adapted to the progress of civilization. I shall attempt to exhibit this most complicated machine, as our history and our laws shew it in action; and not as some celebrated writers have most imperfectly represented it, who have torn out a few of its more simple springs, and, putting them together, miscall them the British constitution. So prevalent, indeed, have these imperfect representations hitherto been, that I will venture to affirm, there is scarcely any subject which has been less treated as it deserved than the government of England. Philosophers of great and merited reputation [27] [Page 70] have told us that it consisted of certain portions of monarchy, aristocracy, and democracy; names which are, in truth, very little applicable, and which, if they were, would as little give an idea of this government, as an account of the weight of bone, of flesh, and of blood in a human body, would be a picture of a living man. Nothing but a patient and minute investigation of the practice of the government in all its parts, and through its whole history, can give us just notions on this important subject. If a lawyer, without a philosophical spirit, be unequal to the examination of this great work of liberty and wisdom, still more unequal is a philosopher without practical, legal, and historical knowledge; for the first may want skill, but the second wants materials. The observations of Lord Bacon on political writers, in general, are most applicable to those who have given us systematic descriptions of the [Page 71] English constitution. "All those who have written of governments have written as philosophers, or as lawyers, *and none as statesmen*. As for the philosophers, they make imaginary laws for imaginary commonwealths, and their discourses are as the stars, which give little light because they are so high." — "*Hæc cognitio ad viros civiles propriè pertinet*," as he tells us in another part of his writings; but unfortunately no experienced philosophical British statesman has yet devoted his leisure to a delineation of the constitution, which such a statesman alone can practically and perfectly know.

In the discussion of this great subject, and in all reasonings on the principles of politics, I shall labour, above all things, to avoid that which appears to me to have been the constant source of political error: I mean the attempt to give an air of system, of simplicity, and of rigorous demonstration, to subjects which do not admit it. The only means by which this could be done, was by referring to a few simple causes, what, in truth, arose from immense and intricate combinations, [Page 72] and successions of causes. The consequence was very obvious. The system of the theorist, disencumbered from all regard to the real nature of things, easily assumed an air of speciousness. It required little dexterity to make his argument appear conclusive. But all men agreed that it was utterly inapplicable to human affairs. The theorist railed at the folly of the world, instead of confessing his own; and the men of practice unjustly blamed philosophy, instead of condemning the sophist. The causes which the politician has to consider are, above all others, multiplied, mutable, minute, subtile, and, if I may so speak, evanescent; perpetually changing their form, and varying their combinations; losing their nature, while they keep their name; exhibiting the most different consequences in the endless variety of men and nations on whom they operate; in one degree of strength producing the most signal benefit; and, under a slight variation of circumstances, the most tremendous mischiefs. They admit indeed of being reduced to theory; but to a theory formed on the most extensive views, of the most [Page 73] comprehensive and flexible principles, to embrace all their varieties, and to fit all their rapid transmigrations; a theory, of which the most fundamental maxim is, distrust in itself, and deference for practical prudence. Only two writers of former times have, as far as I know, observed this general defect of political reasoners; but these two are the greatest philosophers who have ever appeared in the world. The first of them is Aristotle, who, in a passage of his Politics, to which I cannot at this moment turn, plainly condemns the pursuit of a delusive geometrical accuracy in moral reasonings as the constant source of the grossest error. The second is Lord Bacon, who tells us, with that authority of conscious wisdom which belongs to him, and with that power of richly adorning truth from the wardrobe of genius which he possessed above almost all men, "Civil knowledge is conversant about a subject which, above all others, is most immersed in matter, and hardliest reduced to axiom." [28]

[Page 74]

IV. I shall next endeavour to lay open the general principles of civil and criminal laws. On this subject I may with some confidence hope that I shall be enabled to philosophise with better materials by my acquaintance with the law of my own country, which it is the business of my life to practise, and of which the study has by habit become my favourite pursuit.

The first principles of jurisprudence are simple maxims of reason, of which the observance is immediately discovered by experience to be essential to the security of men's rights, and which pervade the laws of all countries. [Page 75] An account of the gradual application of these original principles, first, to more simple, and afterwards to more complicated cases, forms both the history and the theory of law. Such an historical account of the progress of men, in reducing justice to an applicable and practical system, will enable us to trace that chain, in which so many breaks and interruptions are perceived by superficial observers, but which in truth inseparably, though with many dark and hidden windings, links together the security of life and property with the most minute and apparently frivolous formalities of legal proceeding. We shall perceive that no human foresight is sufficient to establish such a system at once, and that, if it were so established, the occurrence of unforeseen cases would shortly altogether change it; that there is but one way of forming a civil code, either consistent with common sense, or that has ever been practised in any country, namely, that of gradually building up the law in proportion as the facts arise which it is to regulate. We shall learn to appreciate the merit of vulgar objections against the subtlety and [Page 76] complexity of laws. We shall estimate the good sense and the gratitude of those who reproach lawyers for employing all the powers of their mind to discover subtle distinctions for the prevention of injustice; [29] and we shall at once perceive that laws ought to be neither more *simple* nor more *complex* than the state of society which they are to govern, but that they ought exactly to correspond to it. Of the two faults, however, the excess of simplicity would certainly be the greatest; for laws, more complex than are necessary, would only produce embarrassment; whereas laws more simple than the affairs which they regulate would occasion a defect of justice. More understanding [30] has perhaps been in this manner exerted to fix the rules of life than [Page 77] in any other science; and it is certainly the most honourable occupation of the understanding, because it is the most immediately subservient to general safety and comfort. There is not, in my opinion, in the whole compass of human affairs, so noble a spectacle as that which is displayed in the progress of jurisprudence; where we may contemplate the cautious and unwearied exertions of a succession of wise men through a long course of ages; withdrawing every case as it arises from the dangerous power of discretion, and subjecting it to inflexible rules; extending the dominion of justice and reason, and gradually contracting, within the narrowest possible limits, the domain of brutal force and of arbitrary will. This subject has been treated with such dignity by a writer who is admired by all mankind for his eloquence, but who is, if possible, still more admired by all competent judges for his philosophy; [Page 78] a writer, of whom I may justly say, that he was "*gravissimus et dicendi et intelligendi auctor et magister*;" that I cannot refuse myself the gratification of quoting his words: — "The science of jurisprudence, the pride of the human intellect, which, with all its defects, redundancies, and errors, is the collected reason of ages combining the principles of original justice with the infinite variety of human concerns." [31]

I shall exemplify the progress of law, and illustrate those principles of universal justice on which it is founded, by a comparative review of the two greatest civil codes that have been hitherto formed—those of Rome and of England; [32] of their agreements and disagreements, both in general provisions, [Page 79] and in some of the most important parts of their minute practice. In this part of the course, which I mean to pursue with such detail as to give a view of both codes, that may perhaps be sufficient for the purposes of the general student, I hope to convince him that the laws of civilised nations, particularly those of his own, are a subject most worthy of scientific curiosity; that principle and system run through them even to the minutest particular, as really, though not so apparently, as in other sciences, and applied to purposes more important than in any other science. Will it be presumptuous to express a hope, that such an inquiry may not be altogether an useless introduction to that larger and more detailed study of the law of England, which is the duty of those who are to profess and practise that law.

In considering the important subject of [Page 80] criminal law it will be my duty to found, on a regard to the general safety, the right of the magistrate to inflict punishments, even the most severe, if that safety cannot be effectually protected by the example of inferior punishments. It will be a more agreeable part of my office to explain the temperaments which Wisdom, as well as Humanity, prescribes in the exercise of that harsh right, unfortunately so essential to the preservation of human society. I shall collate the penal codes of different nations, and gather together the most accurate statement of the result of experience with respect to the efficacy of lenient and severe punishments; and I shall endeavour to ascertain the principles on which must be founded both the proportion and the appropriation of penalties to crimes.

As to the *law of criminal proceeding*, my labour will be very easy; for on that subject an English lawyer, if he were to delineate the model of perfection, would find that, with few exceptions, he had transcribed the institutions of his own country. The whole subject of my lectures, of which I have now given the outline, [Page 81] may be summed up in, the words of Cicero:—"Natura enim juris explicanda est nobis, eaque ab hominis repetenda naturâ; considerandæ leges quibus civitates regi debeant; tum hæc tractanda, quæ composita sunt et descripta, jura et jussa populorum; in quibus NE NOSTRI QUIDEM POPULI LATEBUNT QUÆ VOCANTUR JURA CIVILIA."— *Cic. de Leg.* lib. i. c. 5.

V. The next great division of the subject is the law of nations, strictly and properly so called. I have already hinted at the general principles on which this law is founded. They, like all the principles of natural jurisprudence, have been more happily cultivated, and more generally obeyed, in some ages and countries than in others; and, like them, are susceptible of great variety in their application, from the character and usages of nations. I shall consider these principles in the gradation of those which are necessary to any tolerable intercourse between nations; those which are essential to all well-regulated and mutually advantageous intercourse; and those which are highly conducive to the preservation [Page 82] of a mild and friendly intercourse between civilised states. Of the first class, every understanding acknowledges the necessity, and some traces of a faint reverence for them are discovered even among the most barbarous tribes; of the second, every well-informed man perceives the important use, and they have generally been respected by all polished nations; of the third, the great benefit may be read in the history of modern Europe, where alone they have been carried to their full perfection. In unfolding the first and second class of principles, I shall naturally be led to give an account of that law of nations, which, in greater or less perfection, regulated the intercourse of savages, of the Asiatic empires, and of the ancient republics. The third brings me to the consideration of the law of nations, as it is now acknowledged in Christendom. From the great extent of the subject, and the particularity to which, for reasons already given, I must here descend, it is impossible for me, within any moderate compass, to give even an outline of this part of the course. It comprehends, [Page 83] as every reader will perceive, the principles of national independence, the intercourse of nations in peace, the privileges of embassadors and inferior ministers, the commerce of private subjects, the grounds of just war, the mutual duties of belligerent and neutral powers, the limits of lawful hostility, the rights of conquest, the faith to be observed in warfare, the force of an armistice, of safe conducts and passports, the nature and obligation of alliances, the means of negotiation, and the authority and interpretation of treaties of peace. All these, and many other most important and complicated subjects, with all the variety of moral reasoning, and historical examples, which is necessary to illustrate them, must be fully examined in this part of the lectures, in which I shall endeavour to put together a tolerably complete practical system of the law of nations, as it has for the last two centuries been recognised in Europe.

"*Le droit des gens* est naturellement fondé sur ce principe, que les diverses nations doivent se faire, dans la paix, le plus de bien, [Page 84] et dans la guerre le moins de mal, qu'il est possible, sans nuire à leurs véritables intérêts."

"L'objet de la guerre c'est la victoire; celui de la victoire la conquête; celui de la conquête la conservation. De ce principe et du précédent, doivent dériver toutes les loix qui forment *le droit des gens*."

"Toutes les nations ont un droit des gens; les *Iroquois* même qui mangent leurs prisonniers en ont un. Ils envoient et reçoivent des embassades; ils connoissent les droits de la guerre et de la paix: le mal est que ce droit des gens n'est pas fondé sur les vrais principes." *De l'Esprit des Loix*, liv. i. c. 3.

VI. As an important supplement to the practical system of our modern law of nations, or rather as a necessary part of it, I shall conclude with a survey of the *diplomatic and conventional law of Europe*; of the treaties which have materially affected the distribution of power and territory among the European states; the circumstances which gave rise to them, the changes which they effected, and the principles which they introduced into the public code of the Christian [Page 85] commonwealth. In ancient times the knowledge of this conventional law was thought one of the greatest praises that could be bestowed on a name loaded with all the honours that eminence in the arts of peace and of war can confer:

"Equidem existimo, judices, cùm in omni genere ac varietate artium, etiam illarum, quæ sine summo otio non facilè discuntur, Cn. Pompeius excellat, singularem quandam laudem ejus et præstabilem esse scientiam, *in fæderibus, pactionibus, conditionibus, populorum, regum, exterarum nationum*: in universo denique bellijure ac pacis."—*Cic. Orat. pro L. Corn. Balbo*, c. 6.

Information on this subject is scattered over an immense variety of voluminous compilations; not accessible to every one, and of which the perusal can be agreeable only to very few. Yet so much of these treaties has been embodied into the general law of Europe, that no man can be master of it who is not acquainted with them. The knowledge of them is necessary to negotiators and statesmen; it may sometimes be important to [Page 86] private men in various situations in which they may be placed; it is useful to all men who wish either to be acquainted with modern history, or to form a sound judgment on political measures. I shall endeavour to give such an abstract of it as may be sufficient for some, and a convenient guide for others in the farther progress of their studies. The treaties, which I shall more particularly consider, will be those of Westphalia, of Oliva, of the Pyrenees, of Breda, of Nimeguen, of Ryswick, of Utrecht, of Aix-la-Chapelle, of Paris (1763), and of Versailles (1783). I shall shortly explain the other treaties, of which the stipulations are either alluded to, confirmed, or abrogated in those which I consider at length. I shall subjoin an account of the diplomatic intercourse of the European powers with the Ottoman Porte, and with other princes and states who are without the pale of our ordinary federal law; together with a view of the most important treaties of commerce, their principles, and their consequences.

As an useful appendix to a practical [Page 87] treatise on the law of nations, some account will be given of those tribunals which in different countries of Europe decide controversies arising out of that law; of their constitution, of the extent of their authority, and of their modes of proceeding; more especially of those courts which are peculiarly appointed for that purpose by the laws of Great Britain.

Though the course, of which I have sketched the outline, may seem to comprehend so great a variety of miscellaneous subjects, yet they are all in truth closely and inseparably interwoven. The duties of men, of subjects, of princes, of law-givers, of magistrates, and of states, are all parts of one consistent system of universal morality. Between the most abstract and elementary maxim of moral philosophy, and the most complicated controversies of civil or public law, there subsists a connexion which it will be the main object of these lectures to trace. The principle of justice, deeply rooted in the nature and interest of man, pervades the whole system, and is discoverable in every part of it, even to its minutest ramification in a legal [Page 88] formality, or in the construction of an article in a treaty.

I know not whether a philosopher ought to confess, that in his inquiries after truth he is biased by any consideration; even by the love of virtue. But I, who conceive that a real philosopher ought to regard truth itself chiefly on account of its subserviency to the happiness of mankind, am not ashamed to confess, that I shall feel a great consolation at the conclusion of these lectures, if, by a wide survey and an exact examination of the conditions and relations of human nature, I shall have confirmed but one individual in the conviction, that justice is the permanent interest of all men, and of all commonwealths. To discover one new link of that eternal chain by which the Author of the universe has bound together the happiness and the duty of his creatures, and indissolubly fastened their interests to each other, would fill my heart with more pleasure than all the fame with which the most ingenious paradox ever crowned the most eloquent sophist.

I shall conclude this Discourse in the noble [Page 89] language of two great orators and philosophers, who have, in a few words, stated the substance, the object, and the result of all morality, and politics, and law.

"Nihil est quod adhuc de republicâ putem dictum, et quo possim longius progredi, nisi sit confirmatum, non modo falsum esse illud, sine injuriâ non posse, sed hoc verissimum, sine summâ justitiâ rempublicam regi non posse."—*Cic. Frag.* lib. ii. *de Repub.*

"Justice is itself the great standing policy of civil society, and any eminent departure from it, under any circumstances, lies under the suspicion of being no policy at all."—*Burke's Works*, vol. iii. p. 207.

FOOTNOTES

[1]Syllabus of Lectures on the Law of England, to be delivered in Lincoln's-Inn Hall by M. Nolan, Esq. London, 1796. Back to text

[2] I have not been deterred by some petty incongruity of metaphor from quoting this noble sentence. Mr. Hume had, perhaps, this sentence in his recollection, when he wrote a remarkable passage of his works. See Hume's Essays, vol. ii. p. 352. ed. Lond. 1788. Back to text

[3] The learned reader is aware that the "jus naturæ" and "jus gentium" of the Roman lawyers are phrases of very different import from the modern phrases, "law of nature" and "law of nations." "Jus naturale," says Ulpian, "est quod natura omnia animalia docuit." D. I. I. I. 3. "Quod naturalis ratio inter omnes homines constituit, id que apud omnes peræque custoditur vocaturque jus gentium." D. I. I. 9. But they sometimes neglect this subtle distinction—"Jure naturali quod appellatur jus gentium." I. 2. I. II. *Jus feciale* was the Roman term for our law of nations. "Belli quidem æquitas sanctissimè populi Rom. feciali jure perscripta est." Off. I. II. Our learned civilian Zouch has accordingly entitled his work, "De Jure Feciali, sive de *Jure inter Gentes*." The Chancellor D'Aguesseau, probably without knowing the work of Zouch, suggested that this law should be called, "*Droit entre les Gens*," (Œuvres, tom. ii. p. 337.) in which he has been followed by a late ingenious writer, Mr. Bentham, Princ. of Morals and Pol. p. 324. Perhaps these learned writers do employ a phrase which expresses the subject of this law with more accuracy than our common language; but I doubt whether innovations in the terms of science always repay us by their superior precision for the uncertainty and confusion which the change occasions. Back to text

[4] This remark is suggested by an objection of *Vattel*, which is more specious than solid. See his Prelim. § 6. Back to text

[5] "Est quidem vera lex, recta ratio, *naturæ congruens*, diffusa in omnes, constans, sempiterna, quæ vocet ad officium jubendo, vetando à fraude deterreat, quæ tamen neque probos frustra jubet aut vetat, neque improbos jubendo aut vetando movet. Huic legi neque obrogari fas est, neque derogari ex hac aliquid licet, neque

tota abrogari potest. Nec verò aut per senatum aut per populum solvi hac lege possumus. Neque est quærendus explanator aut interpres ejus alius. Nec erit alia lex Romæ, alia Athenis, alia nunc, alia posthac, sed et omnes gentes et omni tempore una lex et sempiterna, et immortalis continebit, unusque erit communis quasi magister et imperator omnium Deus. Ille legis hujus inventor, disceptator, lator, cui qui non parebit *ipse se fugiet et naturam hominis aspernabitur*, atque hoc ipso luet maximas p[oe]nas etiamsi cætera supplicia quæ putantur effugerit."—*Fragm.* lib. iii. *Cicer. de Republ. apud Lactant.*

It is impossible to read such precious fragments without deploring the loss of a work which, for the benefit of all generations, *should* have been immortal. Back to text

[6] "Age verò urbibus constitutis ut fidem colere et justitiam retinere discerent et aliis parere suâ voluntate consuescerent, ac non modò labores excipiendos communis commodi causâ sed etiam vitam amittendam existimarent; qui tandem fieri potuit nisi homines ea quæ ratione invenissent eloquentiâ persuadere potuissent."—*Cic. de Inv. Rhet.* lib. i. in proëm. Back to text

[7]Δικαίωματα των πολεμων Back to text

[8] Cujacius, Brissonius, Hottomannus, &c. &c.—Vide *Gravina Orig. Jur. Civil.* pp. 132-38. edit. Lips. 1737.

Leibnitz; a great mathematician as well as philosopher, declares that he knows nothing which approaches so near to the method and precision of geometry as the Roman law.—*Op.* tom. iv. p. 254. Back to text

[9] Proavia juris civilis.—*De Jur. Bell. ac Pac. Proleg.* § 16. Back to text

[10] Dr. Paley, Princ. of Mor. and Polit. Philos. Pref. pp. xiv. and xv. Back to text

[11] Grot. Jur. Bell. et Pac. Proleg. § 40. Back to text

[12] I do not mean to impeach the soundness of any part of Puffendorff's reasoning founded on moral entities. It may be explained in a manner consistent with the most just philosophy. He used, as every writer must do, the scientific language of his own time. I only

assert that, to those who are unacquainted with ancient systems, his philosophical vocabulary is obsolete and unintelligible. Back to text

[13] I cannot prevail on myself to pass over this subject without paying my humble tribute to the memory of Sir W. Jones, who has laboured so successfully in Oriental literature, whose fine genius, pure taste, unwearied industry, unrivalled and almost prodigious variety of acquirements, not to speak of his amiable manners and spotless integrity, must fill every one who cultivates or admires letters with reverence, tinged with a melancholy which the recollection of his recent death is so well adapted to inspire. I hope I shall be pardoned if I add my applause to the genius and learning of Mr. Maurice, who treads in the steps of his illustrious friend, and who has bewailed his death in a strain of genuine and beautiful poetry, not unworthy of happier periods of our English literature. Back to text

[14] Especially those chapters of the third book, entitled, *Temperamentum circa Captivos*, &c. &c. Back to text

[15] Natura enim juris explicanda est nobis, *eaque ab hominis repetenda naturâ.*—*Cic. de Leg.* lib i. c. 5. Back to text

[16] Est autem virtus nihil aliud quam in se perfecta atque ad summum perducta natura.—*Cic. de Leg.* lib. i. c. 8. Back to text

[17] Search's Light of Nature, by Abraham Tucker, esq., vol. i. pref. p. xxxiii. Back to text

[18] Bacon, Dign. and Adv. of Learn. book ii. Back to text

[19] See on this subject an incomparable fragment of the first book of Cicero's Economics, which is too long for insertion here, but which, if it be closely examined, may perhaps dispel the illusion of those gentlemen, who have so strangely taken it for granted, that Cicero was incapable of exact reasoning. Back to text

[20] This progress is traced with great accuracy in some beautiful lines of Lucretius:

— — Mulier conjuncta viro concessit in unum,
castaque privatæ veneris connubia læta
cognita sunt, prolemque ex se vidère coortam:
tum genus humanum primum mollescere cœpit.
— — puerisque parentum
Blanditiis facile ingenium fregere superbum.
Tunc et amicitiam cœperunt jungere habentes
Finitima inter se, nec lædere nec violare.
Et pueros commendârunt muliebreque sêclum
Vocibus et gestu cum balbè significarent
Imbecillorum esse æquum miserier omnium.
Lucret. lib. v. 1. 1010-22.
Back to text

[21] The introduction to the first book of Aristotle's Politics is the best demonstration of the necessity of political society to the well-being, and indeed to the very being, of man, with which I am acquainted. Having shewn the circumstances which render man necessarily a social being, he justly concludes, "Και ότι Φυσει ανθρωπος πολιτικον ζωον "—*Arist. de Rep.* lib. i.

The same scheme of philosophy is admirably pursued in the short, but invaluable fragment of the sixth book of Polybius, which describes the history and revolutions of government. Back to text

[22] To the weight of these great names let me add the opinion of two illustrious men of the present age, as both their opinions are combined by one of them in the following passage: "He (Mr. Fox) always thought any of the simple unbalanced governments bad; simple monarchy, simple aristocracy, simple democracy; he held them all imperfect or vicious, all were bad by themselves; the composition alone was good. These had been always his principles, in which he agreed with his friend, Mr. Burke."—*Mr. Fox on the Army Estimates*, 9th Feb. 1790.

In speaking of both these illustrious men, whose names I here join, as they will be joined in fame by posterity, which will forget their temporary differences in the recollection of their genius and their friendship, I do not entertain the vain imagination that I can add to their glory by any thing that I can say. But it is a gratification to me to give utterance to my feelings; to express the profound veneration with which I am filled for the memory of the one, and the warm affection which I cherish for the other, whom no one ever heard in public without admiration, or knew in private life without loving. Back to text

[23] *Privilege*, in Roman jurisprudence, means the *exemption* of one individual from the operation of a law. Political privileges, in the sense in which I employ the terms, mean those rights of the subjects of a free state, which are deemed so essential to the well-being of the commonwealth, that they are *excepted* from the ordinary discretion of the magistrate, and guarded by the same fundamental laws which secure his authority. Back to text

[24] See an admirable passage on this subject in Dr. Smith's Theory of Moral Sentiments, vol. ii. pp. 101-112, in which the true doctrine of reformation is laid down with singular ability by that eloquent and philosophical writer.—See also Mr. Burke's Speech on Economical Reform; and Sir M. Hale on the Amendment of Laws, in the collection of my learned and most excellent friend, Mr. Hargrave, p. 248. Back to text

[25] Pour former un gouvernement modéré, il faut combiner les puissances, les régler, les tempérer, les faire agir, donner pour ainsi dire un lest à l'une pour la mettre en état de résister à une autre, c'est un chef-d'[oe]uvre de législation que le hasard fait rarement, et que rarement on laisse faire à la prudence. Un gouvernement despotique au contraire saute pour ainsi dire aux yeux; il est uniforme partout: comme il ne faut que des passions pour l'établir tout le monde est bon pour cela.—*Montesquieu, de l'Esprit des Loix*, liv. v. c. 14. Back to text

[26] Lord Bacon, Essay xxiv. Of Innovations. Back to text

[27] The reader will perceive that I allude to Montesquieu, whom I never name without reverence, though I shall presume, with humility, to criticise his account of a government which he only saw at a

distance. Back to text

[28] This principle is expressed by a writer of a very different character from these two great philosophers; a writer, "*qu'on n'appellera plus philosophe, mais qu'on appellera le plus éloquent des sophistes,*" with great force, and, as his manner is, with some exaggeration.

Il n'y a point de principes abstraits dans la politique. C'est une science des calculs, des combinaisons, et des exceptions, selon les lieux, les tems, et les circonstances.—*Lettre de Rousseau au Marquis de Mirabeau.*

The second proposition is true; but the first is not a just inference from it. Back to text

[29] The casuistical subtleties are not perhaps greater than the subtleties of lawyers; *but the latter are innocent, and even necessary.*—Hume's *Essays*, vol. ii. p. 558. Back to text

[30] "Law," said Dr. Johnson, "is the science in which the greatest powers of understanding are applied to the greatest number of facts." Nobody, who is acquainted with the variety and multiplicity of the subjects of jurisprudence, and with the prodigious powers of discrimination employed upon them, can doubt the truth of this observation. Back to text

[31] Burke's Works, vol. iii. p. 134. Back to text

[32] On the intimate connexion of these two codes, let us hear the words of Lord Holt, whose name never can be pronounced without veneration, as long as wisdom and integrity are revered among men:—"Inasmuch *as the laws of all nations are doubtless raised out of the ruins of the civil law,* as all governments are sprung out of the ruins of the Roman empire, it must be owned *that the principles of our law are borrowed from the civil law,* therefore grounded upon the same reason in many things."—12 *Mod.* 482. Back to text

FINIS.

J. MOYES, TOOK'S COURT, CHANCERY LANE.